ADMINISTRATIVE AND FINANCE TIPS FOR THE SMALL BUSINESS

Introduction

This document is dedicated to all entrepreneurs, contains various concepts of administration and finance addressed in a simple and informal way, to bring knowledge to people who have a micro or small Company or that they are willing to start a small business. In terms of administration, different aspects of organizational behavior, motivation, aspects of human resources, logistic, procurement, supplier management, customer analysis, quality, among others, are considered. In relation to the topics of finance, elements of determination of the budget of sales, of purchases, methods of determination of prices. It is important to emphasize that this information is found in various sources of the authors of the theories here considered, however, to professionalize and obtain a higher quality and productivity in the micro and small companies, they are retaken and modified to give a specific approach to theories so that they can be applied by anyone regardless of the size of their company.

Sincerely

Dr. Ma. De los Angeles Mendoza González

Personal attitudes that make your company grow

There are some attitudes that rest on different skills which some people are born with or acquired during their life and that are useful when applied in the Management to consolidate and grow your business. Below are some comments.

Social Skills: Ability to relate to others in such a way that we achieve a maximum of benefits and a minimum of negative consequences, both short and long term, the win-win technique can be applied.

Advanced Skills: These are the ones we use to ask for help, participate, give instructions, follow instructions, apologize, convince others. Useful to create synergy within the company, motivate employees and have an effective direction.

Skills related to feelings: They apply when people know their own feelings, express feelings, understand others 'feelings, confront each other's anger, express affection, resolve fear, self-reward. Allow us to be empathetic, to understand customers, employees and, to maintain an open attitude towards others.

Alternative skills to aggression: They are used to ask for permission, to share something, to help others, to negotiate, to use self-control, to defend their own rights, to respond to jokes. Avoid problems with others, don't get into fights. This skill is very important, because it allows you to reflect before acting impulsively, avoiding confrontations with customers, suppliers and achieving a harmonious environment with employees.

Planning skills: Ability to take initiatives, discern about the cause of a problem, establish a goal, get information, solve problems according to their importance, decide, concentrate on a task. It allows you to prioritize problems and give them the right dimension to "not drown in a glass of water."

Communication skills: The fundamental basis of a healthy relationship between people, so it must be clear and accurate, avoiding unnecessary complexity in the messages transmitted, so that it does not negatively affect interpersonal relationships. It means being clear, and direct, with simple words not to create rumors and to ensure that the instructions and objectives are fulfilled correctly.

Positive self-esteem: They refer to know how to listen, express the messages clearly and accurately, order the thoughts, ability to overcome personal difficulties and acquire commitments, creativity, personal autonomy. With this ability you can have the skill to undertake projects and encourage the creation of more satisfactory social relations.

The important thing about these attitudes is that they can be developed through specialized books and courses to develop self-esteem, conflict management and stress, among others. As well as to through self-criticism and reflection on our shortcomings and search for solutions and constant improvement, serving not only to increase our heritage by solving different conflicts with appropriate attitudes but also to achieve a balance.

Some causes of failure in Micro and small enterprises and how to prevent them

According to statistics, more than 50% of Micro and small businesses close in the first year and around 90% within a period of no more than five years. Below are some of the main causes:

a. Inexperience in managing companies and lack of knowledge of the activity to be done, so it is necessary to request professional advice and training in the activity of the company. This way you can face the problems in that kind of business. The planning phase is important to set the objectives according to the capacity of the Company and set needs to be achieved, to know the strengths, weaknesses, opportunities, and threats of the environment. It is also advisable to assess the changes in the capacities and potentialities of customers, suppliers, current competitors, potential new competitors and suppliers of substitute goods and services.
b. Lack of capital. There is a need to have enough resources to not need loans, and to develop the basic operations that the business requires. Therefore, it is indispensable to have the amount of the monthly fixed expenses, for example for the income of the premises, salaries, electricity, water, among others.
c. Bad location. Verify that there is ease of parking for customers, the characteristics of the environment, competitors, security levels of the place and the number of people passing by.
d. Mismanagement of inventories. Control the items you have and your rotation, because if you don't your

Company can accumulate inputs and products that lead to unnecessary waste and expense.

e. Credit and collection failures. When you sell on credit, you must select convenient customers, establish credit limits, the terms of payment, and manage collections correctly.

Not doing so will lead to the company not having liquidity and not dealing with your fixed expenses or buying inventory.

f. Lack of internal control. Fundamental aspect to avoid internal and external frauds. This is a point that has to do with physical, administrative, and fiscal security.

g. Poor selection of staff and lack of policies or not selecting the appropriate personnel for the development of the activities in the company can lead to losses due to fraud, loss of clients due to poor attention, generating internal problems with the rest of the personnel or directors for disciplinary reasons. Not having policies to select, direct and train staff, it results in the decrease in productivity and employee disloyalty; Determining salaries, rewards, promotions, and training needs will decrease staff turnover, raise productivity levels, and reflect on customer satisfaction and company profits.

h. Centralization in decision-making. The owner becomes a problem for lack of delegation and the time it takes to make decisions, which demotivates the staff and hinders the operations and activities of the company.

i. Get a lot of money out of business for personal expenses. Very common, spend on account or use income generated. The lack of savings leads the company to its destruction.

j) Not knowing oneself. It is essential that the employer recognizes own limitations, capacities, and habitual behaviors in the face of certain circumstances. Recognize them in time will lead you not only avoid mistakes when making decisions, but also act in a way that can cope with the difficult times that every business has.

Therefore, for a company to survive and grow, it is necessary to follow up on the above points and take the corrective measures required at the right time.

Application of the AIDA model to effectively increase sales in companies.

Every merchant must use sales techniques to make known the product or service it offers, regardless of the method of sale being applied. A very effective method of sale is called AIDA, named for its acronyms that refer to: attention, interest, desire, and action.

Below are some sales techniques based on the AIDA model approach:

- Attract Customer attention

Most people have many issues to solve daily, so they do not think about buying something, then the main thing in sales management is to attract the attention of the buyer to what is offered, which implies breaking the indifference. To do this, there are some basic techniques, for example: to make compliments and compliments about your company, office, academic trajectory, skills, or interest in a topic. To thank for the time they invest, for accepting, visiting, or providing attention to the company or product; Arouse curiosity; Present real and honest facts about the benefits that the product or service offers and how it relates to what the customer needs.

- Create and retain customer interest

Once the attention of the prospective buyer has been captured, it is necessary to create an interest in what is offered to retain it long enough to finish the presentation. To do this, it is suggested to help the client identify and recognize that he has a need, desire, or problem, through guiding him with questions regarding what he likes or dislikes the product or service offered, as well as raising a need or problem in third person, referring to the percentage of the population or companies that have the same problem in common.

- Awaken the desire to acquire what is offered.

It refers to helping the customers understand that with the product or service presented to them, they will achieve the satisfaction of their needs or will find the best solution to their problems. Therefore, it is necessary to explain in detail what the product or service does, how it works and additional services. Include such as warranties, delivery times, maintenance, among others; As well as mentioning the important advantages that the product has with respect to another similar one of the competition (not to mention the name) and make use of the strongest benefits that the product offers.

- Bring the customer to the action and close of the sale.

At this point the customer is evaluating the benefits of the product and is comparing to the advantages and disadvantages of acquiring it or not. On the other hand, the seller is considering the time to help the customer decide and persuade him to do so immediately. Here it is advisable to avoid pressing it because if you insist too, there is a chance to irritate the client; So, it's better to establish reasons to buy the item or service based on the benefits it will provide. Finally, it is advisable to point out that the correct use of the steps of this method, will contribute to increase the sales by means of the increase of the desire and the intention of generated purchase.

How to set the right price for items or services? Some methods to establish them.

The price is the monetary value that is allocated to goods or services at the time of selling them. By setting the price, you should always think about the consumers, and how much we believe they would be willing to pay for our products compared to the competition, considering the characteristics of our product or service, its benefits, exclusivity, the identification of the mark, the place of the sale, among other aspects. By having low prices, there is a greater possibility of increasing the number of customers and frequency of purchase, but with the disadvantage that you will have a low profit margin and will need a reduction in costs to be able to survive, as this option is easy to neutralize by the competition and difficult to maintain for a long time.

Some pricing methods are as follows:

Pricing based on cost

The easiest way to set prices is to add a standard amount to the cost of the product. For example, an item is purchased in $200.00 and sold at $300.00, with an increase of 50 percent. The gross margin is $100.00, and if the operating costs are $80.00 per sold item, the profit margin will be $20.00

Cost method plus margin

It is to add a profit margin to the total unit cost of the product. The total unit cost is calculated by adding to the variable cost the total fixed costs divided by the number of units produced, this method simplifies the price determination and facilitates the calculation of any sales or adjustment.

Price method according to the demand

It has a subjective basis, the perceived value of a product by the consumer marks the maximum price limit. When it increases, the demand decreases, and the market may not acquire the minimum volume needed to reach the equilibrium point with the highest price. For example, a company calculates that with its current fixed and variable costs, the price must be $300.00 to reach the desired profits; But market research shows that few consumers will pay more than $250.00. Then the company will have to cut its costs to lower the equilibrium point, so that the price that consumers expect is fixed. These methods try to adapt prices to existing demand; The most common are:

1) Price discrimination. It consists on sell the same product at different prices, depending on the place, time of year in question, among others.
2) Experimentation. Try for a period several prices for the same product and determine how they affect the demand, to fix the most suitable according to the objectives of the company.
3) Intuition. It consists on set prices based on the presumption of the effects that they will have on the demand.
4) Competition-based pricing. It is to set a price that keeps a certain relation with the prices of the competitors. These prices depending on our position in the market will be fixed above, equal or below the competition.

Budget Control, an indispensable tool for the administration of family income.

Like a company, a family can manage their income and expenses through a budget. Below are the basic elements to make a budget to verify that you do not spend more than you can have as real income.

1) Income budget

Relate all income you get monthly, such as: wages, interest, income from any other concept you get.

2) Expenditure budget

Relate all expenses you make monthly, such as: tuition fees, electricity, water, rent, out-of-home meals, telephone, card payment, supermarket, cinema, transportation, fuel, clothing, internet, gifts, cigarettes, etc. It is possible to forget to write down some expenses the first month, so it is advisable to keep track of them for a couple of months to adjust their monthly spending plan.

3) Compare the income budget with the cost estimate and observe the relationship they keep.

Monthly income-monthly expenses = final balance (+ or-)

After comparing income with expenses, there are three possibilities:

A. *Income is consistent with expenses*. In this case there is not much problem, just try to stick to your budget and if you want to make some savings, decrease some concept of spending as soon as possible.
B. *Income exceeds expenses*. That would be the ideal situation. However, it is also important to plan so as

not to squander the surplus income and have an amount for difficult times.

C. *Income is not enough to cover expenses.* It is important to follow a savings plan that reduces expenses and avoids debt to cover expenses.

Some tips that allow you to reduce family spending:

- Cut superfluous expenses: Change cell phone company, internet, refinance car payments, use prepaid cards, cancel club memberships.
- Watch Credit cards: Consolidate accounts, get reduced interest, pay more than minimum.
- Reduce spending on food: Be very clear before leaving home what you are going to buy to make it necessary and not throw away what's left over, check the cheapest products.
- Avoid eating outside: Bring lunch to work, bring home coffee. About clothes, try to make the most of the garments and if there are small children, reassign the garments from the largest to the smallest. Repair shoes, handbags, and backpacks instead of buying new ones. Find cheaper diversions: Go to the movies in the mornings, rent movies to see at home or lend it in the library.

Remember that in the present times there is no guarantee of having a well-paid job, so you should start thinking about how to reduce family expenses and determine if they are necessary to reach the end of the month without economic pressures, achieve some now and, thus have a better future.

Quality questionnaire for micro and small business.

Quality is to make things right and at first, in our environment it is very common to think that quality is mainly for medium and large companies. However, the quality must be applied to all companies, because otherwise they will be destined to disappear because they are not able to compete with others that have higher standards of compliance and organization.

Below is a mini questionnaire that you can apply to your company to know the current situation of the same.

There are five sentences from which you should select the one that most fits your environment. It is rated from 0 to 4, where: (0) is practically not performed, (1) is partially performed (sometimes), (2) is usually performed (in most cases), (3) is carried out systematically and in almost all areas, (4) is always carried out and, in total form and, we are an example for the sector.

To get your total score count the results and multiply by the points that indicate, add them up and get the total points. Example: If in question 1 and 2 – you qualified 2, you will add 2 questions and multiply them by the value 2 and your result is 4.

Questionnaire:

1. The company is managed according to the Total quality, and are an example for other companies in the sector
2. Recognizes the achievements and commitment of people and teams who strive to improve.
3. The staff knows the plans and objectives of the company, and by agreement with the management

they transform them into their own objectives and they are provided with the means to enable them to fulfil them.

4. Plans are made for staff (admission, training, development, etc.) evaluating the performance and development needs of all people.

5. There is an effective upward, downward, and inter-personnel communication, participating in a real way in the improvement activities.

6. Efficient financing is available by controlling key financial parameters and using financial resources to support the organization's plans.

7. Supplier selection and evaluation is systematically managed.

8. Customer-oriented processes are being obtained and the degree of satisfaction measured.

9. They have a system to measure customer satisfaction through surveys or similar where aspects such as quality, deliveries, flexibility, communication, etc. are included.

10. They also use other indicators to measure customer satisfaction such as company image, claims level, customer loyalty, etc.

11. The measures are performed in a systematic way, the satisfaction of the staff considering their needs and expectations such as working environment, possibility of promotion, communication, training, recognition, etc.

12. They are also used to measure staff satisfaction rate of absenteeism, rotation, etc.

13. The results and trends of the other indicators used in the company are generally positive.

Results:

a) Less than 20 points obtained: they are far from the Total Quality and have a long way to approach it. It is suggested that they begin by implanting their administrative control system.

b) Between 20 and 30 points obtained: They have advanced their way towards the Total Quality. It is suggested acting on the topics with the lowest score and establishing a plan of action with priorities.

c) between 31 and 45 points obtained: Their tendency towards Total Quality is very positive. It is suggested to analyze its salient points and apply similar measures to the subjects with the lowest score.

d) More than 46 points obtained:
Your company is managed according to the Total Quality and it is an example for other companies in the sector.

Determination of credit policies in a company

Currently it is very important to have a good management of accounts receivable in a company, especially when your product is not easily acquired in a single exhibition by most people, but because of the price it requires to be liquidated in instalments, or to the competition that obliges them to give credit.

Given this situation, if you do not establish a credit policy with probability sales will be less than expected, so it is essential to consider the following aspects to have a portfolio of accounts receivable healthy:

Minimum criteria for granting credit to a customer:

a) Credit evaluations: It is to realize the real situation of our client, both economically and financially, as well as his responsibilities of payment.

To evaluate credit applications:

1) Use the sources of information: Financial statements, ratings and credit reports, bank research, commercial references, company experience.
2) Analyze credit. With the information collected the client's solvency is determined, the liquidity of the applicant and his capacity to pay on time are considered.
3) Make the decision and line of credit. The line of credit is the maximum limit allowed by the company.

b) It is also important to note that flexible credit standards increase office expenses, portfolio management costs, as well as the likelihood or risk of acquiring a hard-to-collect account, but it also increases sales volume in the company.

Establishing flexible credit standards requires analyzing the difference between what It is hard to keep accounts receivable and what you get from additional utility for sales on credit, that is if you have increased sales.

C.   Collection procedures and policies.

Letter shipments, phone calls, personal visits, lawsuits are usually used.
The factors that determine a good management of the collection Policy are: The quality of the account accepted, the duration of the credit period, the percentage of discount for soon payment, level of expenses of collection.
As noted above, a collection policy tailored to the characteristics of the company will generate an improvement in sales and ensure a better rate of recovery of the portfolio.

Diagnosis of training needs in organizations

Training is a constant process in an organization regardless of the activity it performs or its size. In addition to the initial training of a job, it is important to analyze situations that require identifying the training needs of employees by areas of work to fulfill their mission, to perform their duties or execute projects.

As a means of diagnosing training needs, among others, the following are used: observations, requests for management, interviews, surveys, analysis of gaps between the actual and ideal profile, performance evaluation results, update of cargo descriptions, improvement processes.

In addition to the diagnosis, some indicators can sometimes be detected in the Company that indicate possible training needs, such as the following:

A) A priori: Before they happen (when the company decides to make some changes, it should also think about the impact on human capital):

- New Employee income
- Reduction in number of employees
- Process changes and working methods
- Faults, licenses, or staff vacations
- Changes in work and production programs
- Modernization of equipment, machinery, applications, information systems

B) A Posteriori (when the company's operation presents the following):
   1. Production problems:
- Breakdowns in equipment and installations
- Faulty communications

- Excessive costs in maintenance of equipment and machinery
- Excess errors and waste
  2. Staff problems

- Poor staff relationships
- Excessive number of complaints
- Little or no interest in the work
- Faults and frequent substitutions
- Errors in execution of orders
- Deficient organizational climates

It is therefore important for organizations to be aware of the training needs of workers, as it represents an opportunity to increase revenues by to have personnel that is efficiently fulfilling the objectives of the company, or it can be cause of financial problems when there is rubbish, dissatisfaction of clients, among others, because they have not been made an adequate diagnosis about.

Facing the future through personal strategic planning.

Alvin Toffler assures that the best way to predict the future is to invent it, while Peter Drucker says that strategic management is "... do well what needs to be done, because there is nothing more frustrating for the human being than doing what is good for nothing."

The previous statements of gurus of the strategic business Administration can also be applied in a personal way, so the following reflections are presented below:

A.   They refer to the future to be planned, i.e. to make scenarios about how the different decisions taken or situations that confront each other can affect us. There are internal threats, such as excessive spending either generated by impulsive purchases or by real needs and external threats, for example the reduction of deductible expenses by the Treasury, which will generate higher taxes, or the inflation that can be generate and affect purchasing power by having the same wage and price increase.

B. Doing nothing reduces our range of man oeuvre, that is, to react to events that may happen whether they are known.

C. Then, it is necessary to plan, to make an analysis about what I have, what I owe, the normal and extraordinary income (like the bonus), and to make the decisions that are more convenient, ask yourself what's best for you to pay your debts, if you have them, buy now is better than postpone the purchase?, are there conditions for you to liquidate the agreed deadlines?

D. Having a healthy life economically is synonymous with a better quality of life; Therapists, psychologists and experts in the field assure that in time of crisis, the most advisable is to return to the basics, or if we compared it with a company is to do more with less,

E. Reduce superfluous expenses, keep the useful life of the assets as far as possible. Doing things well means lowering costs, saving energy and focusing on what makes us useful, which does not always refer to the material aspect, but can get the same satisfaction without being onerous, for example: If you like to read but have decided that it is one of the concepts of deductions that will reduce to try to save, then you can consult other options, you should not necessarily give up the pleasure that provides a good book. For example, you can go to the book fairs where there are very economic specimens and sometimes barter or exchange is used;

Another way is to set up a reading club with friends and acquaintances who share the same hobby, attend a library, and borrow a book or simply download a book online.

It is important to remember that plans are the result of the planning process and can be defined as detailed designs or schematics of what will be done in the future, and the specifications necessary to make them; It should be planned to achieve the objectives arise. Every person like an organization must consider objectives, not to waste time, to know clearly where you want to go, you want to do and avoid as Drucker says, frustration and fatigue to realize that time and effort has been invested in do something right without we knew exactly why we did it

Internal control in Micro and small enterprises.

In large and medium-sized enterprises, different methods and procedures are implemented to continually review internal control and thus safeguard their assets, verify the accuracy of finances, and streamline their operations. In the Micro and Small business usually only, physical inventories of goods are made, if the staff handles cash bails are requested or a cash transport service is contracted to a specialized company, among other measures of internal control that are carried out.

However, internal control goes further, because if it is done properly it will guarantee the protection of the company's patrimony, through establishing measures that protect its assets, finances and ensure compliance with tax and labor standards, giving the managers the freedom to dedicate themselves to planning and making decisions that contribute to their consolidation in the market.

The following aspects are considered basic internal control tests for any company:

A. Physical controls over assets. Check if the furniture and equipment is inventoried and has a control number, if there are letters of responsibility signed by employees who have assigned vehicles and computer equipment, collate if they have assets invoice files and if they are insured.

B. Goods. Verify if they are physically protected, if there is a responsible storekeeper, collates and signature of authorized exit and entry orders.

C. To verify if there are planning systems and information reports that establish the objectives of the administration, such as: Organization handbooks, procedural manuals, budgets, forecasts, financial reports, bank reconciliations, documentary review of collection, tracking the seniority of balance of accounts receivable and payable.

D. Verification of the fulfillment of tax obligations, revision of the file of provisional payments presented, calculation of taxes, annual declarations, fulfillment of labor obligations and in case of fines or information requirements.

E. Verification of personnel policies and practices They include procedures and policies for hiring, training, evaluating, promoting, and compensating employees, as well as providing them with the necessary resources to meet the assigned responsibilities.

If the analysis of the company is found to be deficient in the controls, it must be corrected to prevent future losses to the patrimony, either by theft, diversion of resources, slowness in the collection, losses due to lack of insurance to fixed assets in case of accidents, penalties for non-compliance with accounting, tax and labor laws, hiring of people who do not have the right profile, among other situations that may affect the company economically.

Customer service in accommodation establishments.
Accommodation establishments are all those that provide the public with services Lodging on a temporary basis and can be classified according to their size, distinctives, capacity, among others.
However, the most important thing for the client is the service and attention that is provided to him when he goes to one of these establishments. Here are some aspects to consider increasing user satisfaction.

1.   Focus on the customer.

- Listen carefully to the customer
- Remain calm in the face of any situation that arises.
- Look at the customer in the face and be attentive to the gestures.
- Answer the questions clearly, accurately, and opportunely.
- Use a proper tone of voice to the situation.
- Show the customer that at that time he is the most important.
- Be aware of the non-verbal communication of the client (gestures, gaze, movement of the body, hands).

2.   Specify the customer's need.

- Formulate questions such as: when, where, who, how, for that.
- Summarize what the customer says to verify its content.
- Check with the If that's the real need

3.   Stimulate the customer.

Address the customer by name
Listen to it avoiding interruptions
Treat the customer as an adult.

4.   Service-centric actions.

- Give explanations: Explain the rules of the establishment and the fundamentals
- Send to Customer: Indicate the person or department that will help the customer in the situation.

5.   Provide an efficient service.
- Respond quickly.
- Formulate precise questions.
- Analyze client/guest responses.
- Provide the service.
- Make sure the customer was satisfied.
- Formulate alternatives to meet the requirements.

It is important to consider that the following working technique should always be considered: to greet and offer help, to listen attentively the approaches, obtain additional information, present different options, establish agreements and execute actions, finally say goodbye and express expectations.

If the above suggestions are put into practice it will surely improve the efficiency in the service and thus elevate the quality and satisfaction of the clients.

Start a business, a profitable option.

Becoming an entrepreneur and starting your own business can be an option for many people, either because they have identified a niche market or because they want to be their own bosses. But how do you do it alone? Here are some tips that can help you.

A) Decide to start. Identify your priorities and decide to start your business. Answer the following questions:

Are you committed to the decisions you take?

Are you willing to work seven days a week and late at night?

Do you see the business as a hobby or a job?

What is your reward and how much do you risk?

What place would you like to take on the competition?

How big is the market in the area in which you intend to venture?

Who are the competitors?
What is your financial model?

B. Build a brand. Design and register your brand to protect your products or services.

C. Determine the geographical location of your establishment. Consider your market, parking, security, access, among others.

Try the online sale. You can have a small place, few employees, little storage, so you will keep the costs at a low level.

Develop an administrative and financial plan.

Examine the legal and fiscal aspects.

Analyze labor obligations.

The skills that every entrepreneur must possess to succeed, are among others:

1) A Vision
2) Will to adapt and be flexible.
3) Determination. Never accept no as an answer, there is always a choice.
4) Communication skills.
5) Knowledge and understanding of cash flows, that is, managing money inflows and exits efficiently.
6) A lot of energy.
7) Take risks.
8) Being patient, business is not successful overnight.

Ability to identify their own personal weaknesses. Be aware of the strengths and weaknesses to confront and improve them.

It is important that you consider the necessary aspects to determine if you have what it takes to start your own business, because if you decide you will get personal benefits, such as managing your time, flexible schedules, not bosses, among others.

Strategist or Manager? Characteristics that distinguish it

Already in 1990, K. Ohmae in his work "The Mind of the strategist" establishes various characteristics that distinguish a strategist, of course, this theory has been extended derived from the use of the technology and the exigencies of the current times.

The manager manages, has a competitive performance, applies technical-scientific knowledge, works as a team, communicates effectively, among other aspects, however, some important aspects that have a strategist and distinguish it from a manager, are:

A. To ensure competitive professional performance, the strategist effectively implements technical-scientific knowledge and modern instrumental tools, speaks other languages, possesses skills and skills, and It must also bring together several additional competencies to enable it to perform efficiently in organizations.

B. Possesses charisma and leadership

   a) He is not satisfied, he hopes more, he is sure of himself, he is critical of himself and others. He knows his strengths and weaknesses and takes advantage of these aspects to build and take advantage of the opportunities presented to him.
   b) Questions, seeks, and suggests changes, which differentiates them from others as most people, on the other hand, tend to expect things to happen.
   c) He is adaptable, versatile, and ready for continuous learning.
   f) He is discrete, compartmentalizing relevant information and communicating it at the right time

and level. In this way, no one can be able to Know their strategy, only tactics and will not be copied.

g) Has a wide culture.

h) Has the capacity to work in teams of different disciplines.
i) Practice empathic communication, it says things directly, trying to improve the working environment.

Also, a strategist is alert to the opportunities that are presented but always with a clear objective, has a sense of direction that allows him to advance and achieve his long-term goals.

Since you always have plans; View options and evaluate scenarios, weighs the costs and benefits of each, "what would happen if...?", "What would be the best course of action...?". So, you can chain an action to another looking to provoke the effect you want.

This ability to visualize allows you to have the ability to respond to unexpected situations.

Finally, it is important to remember that in companies the competitive impact of strategies and their success is because the plans have the creative element, determination and will of the strategist who conceived them.

Business Management Assessment

The evaluation of the business management is an objective, concrete and integral evaluation of the activities that are carried out in an area or a company to fulfil its aims and objectives, among other aspects: to evaluate the effectiveness of the internal policies, norms consistent with its mission, objectives and strategic plans, achievement of the objectives, organizational structure, individual participation of each employee, verification of compliance with general and specific regulations, evaluation of efficiency and economy, measurement of the degree of reliability of the information financial and attention to the existence of ineffective or more costly procedures.

This type of assessment has a comprehensive approach and is considered an economy and efficiency audit. The management comprises the activities of a company that involve the establishment of goals and objectives, as well as the evaluation of its performance and fulfillment of an operational strategy that guarantees the survival and growth of the same.

Stages for the evaluation of business management

The main activities are: data collection, results calculations, analysis of information, the elaboration of conclusions and recommendations.

- Data collection: Basic information on the economic, patrimonial, and global evolution of the company. This information is obtained from the inventory records of warehouse, goods, activities.

- Calculation of results: The core results of the analysis will be net income, equity variation and profitability.

- Analysis of information: The patrimonial analysis concentrates on observing how the company is in terms of its patrimony, its solvency and liquidity to face debts at the end of the management cycle and comparing it with previous situations.

- Global economic Analysis, which is to identify the value of the produced and indigested During the management cycle and the efficiency of this result with respect to invested capitals, how well the management has played and if the decisions that it has taken have contributed to increase profits, decrease waste, lost, or increase productivity.

- Elaboration of conclusions and recommendations: it is important to draw conclusions to identify positive and negative aspects of management and, if necessary, to make recommendations.

This type of evaluation is important in companies, regardless of their size or rotation, because information will be obtained to recapitulate, to obtain conclusions and to modify in their case the decisions that have been taken about the management of the company.

Role of organizational communication

Communication is the set of acts performed by a person through the handling of signs, to bring forth in another an idea or set of ideas that influence the modification or reinforcement of their behavior. On the other hand, communication in the organization is the messages that are exchanged in the scope of a company, between this and its environment.

A. Communication types:

- Formal through a written or informal document through a message, mail, chat, phone, etc.

- Ascending, from subordinate to head immediate or downward (inversely). Between employees of the same rank or departments.

- Internal, only for employees or external when directed to third parties.

- Rumor, Commercial, image, publicity, interpersonal.

B. Media

- Magazine, circulars, notice boards, bulletins.

- Parties, meetings, speeches, ceremonies, values, recognitions.

- Grid, Gossip, among others.

The organizational communication function seeks to develop and implement communication strategies that support the organization in the achievement of its objectives, offering effective coordination resources, supporting the processes of change, reinforcing the Integration of the staff, and collaborating in the maintenance of an optimal reputation and image of the Organization, its members, its practices, and its products. It is important to remember that the communication is a strategic resource for any organization.

Without communication, the existence of the organization is not feasible; Better communication implies better possibilities of reaching the objectives of the Organization.

Three different areas of communication are recognized:

- Institutional: It consists in establishing, strengthening, and preserving the image and positioning of the institution. Some typical activities: media relations, establishing institutional identity (logos, graphic identity), making alliances with related organizations, attending government affairs, carrying out social responsibility programs.
- Marketing: seeks to promote a response, attitude, or behavior among the target audiences. Its activities include developing marketing plans, product/service launches, dissemination of product/service benefits, establishing direct mail, designing didactic campaigns and strategic alliances with media
- Organizational communication: Performs activities of an internal nature. Its activities are the development and strengthening of organizational culture, studies and improvement of the organizational climate, management of change, systematization of internal media, and integration of work teams.

Thus, it is necessary to analyze how the communication process is developing in your company, to verify whether it is contributing to position your product or service and promoting problem solving or the Contrary is creating conflicts because of misuse.

Identify key success factors to improve a company's competitiveness

A company should not only meet the needs of its customers but must do better than its competitors. For this, it requires identifying the key success factors, i.e. the essential areas for the company to achieve the expected results.

Sometimes it is not only the product or service that is offered is the key factor of success, of course it is important the quality of what is offered, however the success of the company can depend on aspects such as distribution, marketing or personnel working in it.

Therefore, it is necessary to know who your client is, what is needed and what you have, for this you can divide the company into three aspects:

- Financial resources
- Technology
- Personal

In the aspect of financial resources, you should ask if you have enough to develop the skills of the staff and the technology, if it is possible to generate them in the medium or long term, if you can obtain the external resources that are required either through Loans, look for new partners, for example.

In technology also known as know-how, you have to determine if you have the necessary technology, whether you can develop or buy licenses to obtain it.

In relation to staff, it is important to analyze whether you have the necessary staff, whether you can train, or if you can get employees with more skills.

On the other hand, competition must also be analyzed to be compared and to determine which capacities require to be developed by the company. Some questions that may be asked are:

- Is your staff better prepared than our company?
- Do you have better technology?
- Is your financial capacity stronger?
- What is recommended in this analysis is to carry out it by departments or areas of the company.

The objective of the previous analyses is to decide what to do in terms of the capabilities develop, with the deficiencies encountered, because if not do it runs the risk of lagging even more with respect to competitors.

Thus, to know what the clients of the company value and the key factors of success, it allows to carry out an analysis of the environment and internal, as well as to reflect on the capacities, human skills, technology, and financial resources that the company requires to Satisfy customers. Therefore, it is imperative to analyze competitors to make operations and processes better than other companies that perform activities like ours.

Importance of statistical data to establish a Micro-enterprise

Any country has a criterion of stratification to establish the size of an enterprise related to the economic censuses. Around the world statistical data indicates the importance of the microenterprise.

Micro-enterprises are responsible to have many workers and contribute to economy.

The importance of the statistical data is not only to show that micro companies represent an important economic force in the country and in the state, but also to use the information they provide.

For example, if you are thinking about self-employed through establishing a micro business:

A) The first question will be to establish what their skills are and what they know about, what they do.

B) With how many financial resources you have or where you can go to apply for funding.

C) Before deciding on the activity to be devoted must verify the competition that exists, and that is where the statistical data provide a clear view of the number of companies that exist dedicated to the same activity, its size and number of employees with which it counts.

D) You can also observe the demand that may exist for other services or purchases of items that are not currently covered or that in other states are already growing. This is called locating a niche market.

Statistical data can also help you to conduct a more specific market research in the municipality in which you are located.

F) If you have already decided, remember to set up a business plan to help you establish Strategies not only for survival but for long-term growth.

G) Meet your tax obligations.
Seek counseling and read articles that can help you make the right decisions.

Importance of effective communication in the organization

It is considered organizational communication to the messages that are exchanged between the organization and its environment. The organizational communication function seeks to develop and implement communication strategies that support the organization in achieving its objectives by offering effective coordination resources, supporting the processes of change, reinforcing the Integration of staff, and collaborating in the maintenance of an excellent reputation and image of the Organization, its members, its practices, and its products.

Communication is a strategic resource for any organization, without communication the existence of the organization is not feasible; Better communication implies better possibilities of reaching the objectives of the Organization. There are three different areas of communication:

Institutional: seeks to establish, strengthen, and preserve the image and positioning of the organization.

Marketing: Aimed at promoting a response, attitude or behavior among customers.

Internal: aimed at creating synergy, and coordination among employees for the benefit of the institution

- Institutional communication, some typical activities: Media relations, institutional identity (logos, graphic identity), alliances with related organizations, governmental affairs, social responsibility programs.

- Marketing Communication. Some typical activities: Marketing plans, product launches/services, dissemination of product/service benefits, direct mail, campaign design, strategic alliances with media.

- Organizational communication. Some typical activities: Development and strengthening of organizational culture, studies and improvement of organizational climate, management of organizational change, systematization of means of Internal communication, integration of work teams.

Communication processes: The communication chief-collaborators can be through teamwork, communication boards, communication skills development activities, social and recreational activities promoting the integration.

- Typical media: Internal magazine, newsletters, circulars, and other forms

- Electronic: Intranet, email, multimedia

- Campaigns

- Posters, blankets, signs, and other forms

- Video

- Notice board (billboards, blackboards, planks)

Finally, remember that no matter the size of your company, because communication is given in any organization, with clients and employees in the first instance, so it is advisable to consider the activities, processes and media described contribute to the achievement of your goals.

The importance of supplier selection to improve the purchasing function.

Usually the purchasing needs in an organization are determined with the study of the purchase-process-output sequence and on the basis of this the reorder point is made, however regardless of the method that is established in the company for the acquisition of raw material or finished products, it is important to consider the following aspects in the selection of suppliers that will reduce costs and improve the purchasing process:

I. Selection of sources of supply. 1) Sector analysis: Identify companies that integrate the sector, product characteristics, industrial classification, if any. 2) Commercial availability: Determine whether it is a standardized product, or custom-made, if it is a manufacturer, distributor. 3) Quantity to buy: It is given from availability, if there is a minimum. 4) Purchase request time. 5) Purchase Purpose: Use for fabrication, components, special or non-repetitive, physical size.

II. Preliminary selection

To use various sources of information, such as: guides, directories, registers, interview with suppliers and direct representatives of factories, catalogues, advertising activity, Magazines. As well as internal source of specialists, archives of suppliers, organizations of specialists/professionals, fairs, exhibitions, samples.

III. Selection of Quotes

According to the number of bidders desired, it must be selected by: competition in price, technological and service competence.

IV. Evaluation of contributions.

Should be considered: required quantities, description and specifications of items, consumer delivery points, delivery time, method and transport prices, delivery dates, contractual considerations, prices, proposals, identification of Contest based on quantity prices, price per periodicity of delivery, period of respect for prices, exceptions, or invalidation of prices for events, low protected price, subject to scale, guarantees, claims, among others.

Finally, it is advisable to comment on what the relationship with suppliers should be based on honesty, sincerity about the virtues of the product, reciprocal knowledge of the product and mutual policies supplier-client (purchase and sale).

Importance of the physical distribution of products.

The distribution relates to the activities that are carried out to generate the best conditions of time, place, and situation in the customer service, since the company must be able to place its products in the indicated place and precise moment.

The most important decision in the field of physical distribution and choice of channels, refers to whether the company carries out or if it needs to delegate it to an agent, among other figures that can provide the service. It is also essential to know the customer to determine their purchasing habits such as:

1) Every time you purchase the product, either the company distributes or a similar or substitute.
2) where you make the purchase, if it is in a place close to your home, in shopping centers, pharmacies or another specific place.

Some distribution strategies for retail companies:

A) to make home delivery of orders made through telephone calls.

B. Create a Web page to offer the products and send them either by parcel or by own transport.

C. To make consignment contracts with different companies, this is to give product to a company or chain of companies that can Display the products without purchasing it, i.e. they will only pay for the products that are sold.
D. Hire sales staff to visit customers, either door-to-door or specialized business where the product is required.

E. Send catalogues with the products to the clients 'domicile, or send it by e-mail, or other existing application in the technological market. Remember to make a database of people who have already purchased their products so that they can periodically communicate with them and send them information about their products.

F. Participate in fairs and exhibitions of products of the same branch or activity, this allows to expose the product to countless people who are potential consumers.

g) Contract an island, or a small space in an important mall, can be for a couple of days or a weekend. Present product information, display, let prospective customers handle, test, or taste your product. Schedule visits, enter addresses, phone numbers, and email to track those who seem interested in your product.

h) Participate in markets on wheels where you can display your product without being very onerous.

Remember that the success of your company can depend on the marketing channels you have implemented, because that way will make available to customers their products in a comfortable and accessible way, which will facilitate the sale of their products and increase Their profits.

.

Importance of establishing credit policies in companies.

The functions of credit in companies are that they increase consumption, encourage the use of goods and services, and allow the expansion and opening of new markets. The main reason most companies offer sales on credit is because their competitors also offer credit.

The management of accounts receivable is designed to coordinate the elements of a company to maximize the equity and reduce the risk of a liquidity and sales crisis through the optimal management of aspects such as commercial credit policies granted to clients and collections strategy.

Credit Policies:

They are the set of activities and decisions that comprise the credit standards of a company, including the methods used to collect the credit accounts and the procedures to control the credit. The objectives of these policies are to reduce to the maximum the investment of accounts receivable, to maintain the investment in accounts receivable to the current, to avoid the overdue portfolio, to monitor the accounts receivable against the inflation and the devaluation.

It is not advisable to have a single client, it must be diversified so that the risks, of lack of collection do not affect the company in an important way. It is important to analyze the credit; A known tool is through the five "C".

b) The five "C" of the credit

1) Character: The applicant's history of fulfilling past obligations.

2) Capacity: The disposition of the applicant to pay the requested credit, determined by means of an analysis of financial statements focused on the cash flows available to establish whether it can comply with the payments of the debt.

3) Capital: The strength of the financial structure of the applicant, evaluating whether it will be able to pay the resources requested according to the income it has.

4) Collateral: The amount of assets that the applicant has available to secure the credit. The greater the amount of assets available, the greater the possibility that a company will recover its funds if the applicant fails to comply with the payment.

5) Conditions: Terms of payment according to the current business situation and the general trends of the country.

Therefore, it is advisable to establish clearly the credit policies so that it can assure as much as possible the recovery of the sales that are made through this medium, since according to the economic conditions of the country it is necessary to use the credit to sell.

Importance of cash control in the internal administrative control of a company.

Internal administrative control consists of taking measures related to operational efficiency and the observation of policies established in the organization, for example: Security measures and restricted access. A weakness of internal control does not necessarily imply that the records are erroneous but if there is a possibility that the financial statements will contain errors.

Cash is the concept that represents the liquidity of the assets that a company owns, it is considered as cash to the currencies, banknotes, cheques, bank drafts, and money deposited in banks.

Management is responsible for avoiding losses due to fraud, theft, guaranteeing the accounting accuracy of income, payments, cash balances, maintaining sufficient balance for payments and emergencies, for that the following can be established:

Controls on Cash:

a) Custody of the assets separate from the transaction log.

b) The registration function must be subdivided into several employees.

For this, the following procedures can be performed:

1) Verify that all income is deposited and timely, by the following day
2) to perform surprise arches, by personnel outside the box area, to check if all the cash received has been posted and if the balance of this account corresponds

to what is physically found in cash, cheques or vouchers.

3) Pay the expenses with checks.

4) A suitable fixed background must be assigned.

5) Verify that all revenues that should be received are received, for example: Call customers who due to verify when they made their last payment and check that they have been entered and registered the corresponding payment.

6) Establish prenumbered forms for income and expenses.

7) Implement an appropriate account plan that allows you to correctly post income and expenses.

8) Establish a system of authorization of expenses and payments.

9) Proper separation of functions between the paying and the recording.

10) Issuing a nominal cheque

With the establishment of the above measures, the following situations can be avoided that may arise to cover funds and generate fraud in the company:

Cancel fictitious expenses, post, and pay false bills, post and pay duplicates of documents, postpone deposits, adulterate documents correcting figures, adulterate the sum of fixed funds reimbursements, use the collection money to make personal payments adulterating the sum of the collections and removing the difference, adulterate deposits and subsequently alter the bank reconciliations, adulterate deposit ballots and Bank debit notes (charges) for equivalent sums.

Therefore, establishing appropriate control measures on your cash will help safeguard your assets and ensure confidence in the controls established by the company.

Importance of emotional intelligence in organizations

Daniel Coleman, an American psychologist, created the concept of emotional intelligence, and refers to the ability to recognize feelings of their own and others.

For Coleman, emotional intelligence implies five basic abilities: discovering emotions and feelings of their own, recognizing them, managing them, creating self-motivation, and managing personal relationships.

Therefore, a person with low emotional intelligence will often be left to carry by his impulses which will bring him problems. However, a person with high emotional intelligence, will not plan all his movements but does have a much more rational and intelligent perspective, and his emotions are unlikely to destabilize him at crucial times and can get the following objectives in their relationship with others:

- That those around you feel comfortable with it.
- When you are at your side do not experience any kind of negative feeling.
- Trust him or her when they require advice on a personal and professional level.

A. Characteristics of a person with emotional intelligence:

- Recognizes and manages negative emotions that you experience.
- has a greater ability to relate to others because empathy has the advantage of understanding them by putting themselves in their positions.
- Manages to use criticism as something positive, as it analyzes and learns from them.

- By channeling negative emotions, you have a greater ability to be happy.
- It has the necessary qualities to cope with adversity and setbacks.

By the foregoing, the organizations require that the emotional intelligence of the workers be encouraged, either through courses or workshops so that they can develop these skills, since in this way the following will be obtained:

a) The worker feels more person, happier, fuller and with greater quality of life;

b) Increases motivation.

c) Improves personal relationships.
d) People develop responsibility and autonomy.

e) The working environment is improved;

f) Reinforces leadership.
g) Increases the efficiency and efficiency of people and equipment;
h) Improves the relationships with the clients and with all the public of the company;
i) Improves the profitability of the company.

Importance of tourist services

The tourist product requires resources, infrastructure, and services. Tourist service is the activity carried out by a physical or moral person, public or private, to satisfy specific needs arising from the tourist displacement. The services also include the symbolic value, psychological, which has to do with the social value that the person assigns, for example: it is necessary to sleep, which is satisfied with a lodging, however the symbolic value that gives the tourist is the fact that want to try a one-or five-star hotel. When launching the product to the market, the tourist product, each one of the existing services must be valued. Generally, the consideration of services includes the following:

A. Basic service It is the reason the customer chooses a tourist product, for example, in the case of a restaurant, it will be the food.

B.   Peripheral services are those that the client has the right to use for being user of the basic service. For example, in the case of the restaurant, it could be the internet, playroom for children.
C.   Complementary services are those that in addition to the above offer an added value with respect to the competition, for example: courtesy cards or food, discounts, daycare, among others.

Among the most important tourist services are the following:
Accommodation: The hotel is categorized from one to five stars. Other: Camping, Timeshare, resort, Bed & Breakfast.

Gastronomy: Includes all kinds of restaurants, bars, cafeteria, etc.

Transport: Plane, cruises, trains, Micros, vans, car rentals, etc.

Tour: Tourism agencies and other tour operators offer a variety of outings accompanied by guides where the most important tourist sites are travelled.

However, the importance of tourism services is assessed as to whether it covers the basic needs and detects the unmet needs of tourists, also generates the economic growth of a place that must go hand of a sustainable development and benefit the whole community.

They can be improved from the public, private and community sectors. Of the public sector, usually it is done by the Secretary of Tourism, through comprehensive plans at the macro level contemplating all sectors involved (Chamber of hotels, gastronomy, traders, tour operators).

From the private sector, through the training of staff, as there is usually a deficiency in this regard, as well as little update on the latest trends in the industry in terms of marketing, architecture, interior design, relationships In improving the quality of services and the correct use of inputs, without neglecting the competitiveness factors of the markets such as cost and production.

Lastly, from the community, through the tourist awareness on the part of the Residents, as it is necessary to consider that through the tourist services can generate employment all year, the profits remain in place, contributes to the development and growth of the community

Importance of organizational culture in the company

Organizational culture is defined as a system of shared purposes and common beliefs that follow the members of an organization and that determines, to a large extent, how they act with each other, in other words is the way things are done in a Company, and comprises values, symbols, rituals, myths and practices of the same.

A.   A culture begins with:

The founders of an organization traditionally have a greater impact on the initial culture of that organization because they have a vision of what the Organization should be. The small size that tends to characterize new organizations further facilitates the imposition of the founders 'vision on all members of the organization.

B. Culture is kept alive through:

- Senior Management. -managers, with what they say, and their behavior establish rules that are filtered down through the organization.
- New employees and socialization. -The employees when they enter the organization are not familiar with their culture, being able to get to disturb the beliefs and customs that are already established. Therefore, it is necessary that they adapt to the culture through the process of socialization, which includes:

    1) Histories. -Stories circulating in organizations and usually contain a narration of events about the founders of the organization, as the company started, the obstacles they encountered, anecdotes. These stories anchor the present in the

past and provide explanations and legitimacy to current practices.

2) Rituals. - Repetitive sequences of activities that express and reinforce the key values of the organization, indicate that goals are more important, that people are important and who is not.

3) Material symbols. -These material symbols communicate to the employees who is important, the degree of egalitarianism desired by the high-level management and the kind of behavior that is appropriate. Those are manifested as dress codes, cards presentation, private parking places, among others.

4) Language. -Many organizations and units within them use language as a way of identifying the members of a culture. By learning this language, members demonstrate their acceptance and help preserve it. For example, the use of codes, diminutives.

C. Benefits of organizational culture:

- Creates a stronger commitment of employees to the organization.
- Assists in the recruitment and socialization of new employees.
- Drives greater organizational performance by inculcating and promoting employee initiative.
  It is therefore a good idea to consider whether your company performs some of the activities to strengthen the organizational culture or in your case begin to implement it.

Importance of the budget in the company.

A budget is an action plan aimed at meeting a planned goal, expressed in securities and financial terms, and must be fulfilled at certain times and under certain conditions, so it can be done in any company, regardless of size or activity It carries out.

The main function of budgets is related to financial Control. Budgets can play both preventive and corrective roles within the organization, compared to what is budgeted with what the company is doing.

The budget phases are:

1. Foresight: Prepare in advance what is convenient to meet the presumed needs in time.
2. Planning: (What and how it will be done). Path to follow with unification and systematization of activities according to their objectives.
3. Organization: (who will). Technical structuring between the functions, levels and activities of the human and material elements of an entity.
4. Coordination or integration: (to be done in order: and in general). Development and harmonious maintenance of the activities.
5. Direction: (Guide for it to be done). Executive function to guide and inspect subordinates.
6. Control: (see that is done). Measures to appreciate whether the objectives and plans are being fulfilled.

Methods for drawing up a budget:

1.-Method based on the opinion of the directors (subjective)

2.-Methods based on the opinion and experience obtained by the sales force (subjective)

3.-Statistical analysis Method (objective).

If you have never made a budget, you should start with a budget for income and expenses or cash, that is to consider the possible income you will have in a short-term (annual) period and the expenses you expect to have, including purchases and taxes to pay. These concepts are compared to control the possible surplus or missing cash that can have monthly.

Remember that the important is to make the necessary decisions to reach the proposed goals or to control the expenses established in each period.

Influence of the personal image in the company

The care of the image and the personal arrangement are becoming increasingly important in the life of the people. Seeing, feeling good and being comfortable with the image is something that makes them feel good.

A company also has an image for which it is recognized and endures in time. The people who work in it as responsible for transmitting the credibility of the products or services they offer, must also transmit a good personal image that is consistent with the corporate image.

The personal image is formed by postures, movements when sitting, walking, and greeting; Tone of voice, hygiene, courtesy, education, and dress-up. It is important to care because it is the first thing that others see, we all project our personality through the image we offer abroad.

Image consultants consider that in companies, personal appearance affects 90% to make decisions. On the other hand, changes in appearance have little value if they are not accompanied by changes in the interior, work with values, attitudes, beliefs and self-esteem.

In thirty seconds, people form an impression of a person based on what they see, the hair, clothes, movements, smiles and the rest of non-verbal communication. Hence the importance of the personal image.

When the message that is transmitted at the visual level is positive, the person facing the front will assume that the other aspects are also positive. But, if the visual message is negative, the new customer may not have an opportunity to convey the information that is desired.

For the above, it is important that all companies have stipulated their "dress code" because everything we choose transmits something, and sometimes can go against the company's policy.

For people who have direct and personal contact with the customer in reception positions, customer service, among others, it is essential to have a uniform set by the company, including specifications about hairstyle, makeup and accessories allowed. In the case of women, it is advisable to avoid showing a lot the physical attributions because thus can divert the attention of the audience from the goals they have.

It is important that the company provides training to its employees, which can consist of image workshops, self-makeup courses, creation of the corporate dress code, courses of philosophy of the company, among others.

Some tips on how to dress, according to the type of situation, can be:

A. If you work in a shop or bazaar, with direct attention to the public, you should dress as you usually do, because if you wear a suit you may create a rejection environment, or, use a simple uniform.

B. If you work with company managers, clothing should be managerial, do not use denim trousers and sneakers.

It is important to remember that as the popular wisdom says, "A picture is worth a thousand words"

The science of Chaos according to Philip Kotler: A growth opportunity for companies.

At present there are more risks for companies than before, this is because the technology and the media have reduced the times and distances, so that the companies and economies of the countries are more globalized and interconnected to each other. To these risks Kotler calls it turbulence and says that companies take measures to counteract them as they increase risks. Consequently, they reduce personnel, decrease costs, among others.

It also states that we should not wait for the "Butterfly effect" to happen in another place so that let us act. Until we are already in a crisis, because the new normal is a sequence of highs and lows in the economy that prevent the prediction with greater degree of certainty. Situation that was not given before, since the companies had good and bad cycles on a regular basis, depending on the policies of the Government and the competitors of the local or national market.

Now companies, regardless of their size, must get used to this changing environment and make the necessary decisions to continue operating. Some important aspects that need to be considered are as follows:

1) A very important aspect of information and interconnectivity is that it means that customers know more quickly what is happening in companies, a poor service or low-quality product generate Comments immediately on the Internet and on the various social networks that exist, so that companies that make

products with inferior quality or provide non-high-level services will disappear faster than before.

2) The use of the Internet also generates an opportunity to communicate with customers, e-mail enables communication and collaboration with consumers. Therefore, it is necessary to have a database

Customers emails to be in constant communication about our products, services, promotions, offers and conduct quality surveys.

3) Improve processes continuously and be prepared with possible scenarios of what could happen under different circumstances and how the company could cope with them and minimize the effects.

Have an attitude of alert to prevent the various situations that could affect us, for example: At the macroeconomic level, the increase of taxes, the exchange rate, among others; At the microeconomic level, direct and indirect competition, local social problems, and other aspects.

So, the science of chaos tells us that we must be in constant motion, improve and be alert to the changes that are being made continuously, to take advantage of the opportunities that are presented and reduce the risks by doing nothing.

The most difficult business decision... close or survive and grow?

There are few entrepreneurs who have managed to maintain and grow their company without having faced difficulties at some point in the existence of it. Today, due to the social problems that have arisen, many micro, small and even medium-sized companies have decided to close their doors and finish their operations, since they have not been able to cope with the low sales and to cover the fixed costs that they have. In addition to this situation, major problems are envisioned with the possible fiscal reforms that will be adopted shortly and that much of the business will have to cope.

Given this panorama, it is important that before deciding about the future of your business, discuss the following aspects:

a) Location. Is it well located, how much does the place in your sales contribute? Changing places could help you Getting new customers and if you mention it in advance and gives you a loyalty discount bonus, you can keep the rest of your clientele.

b) Waste. Check the process of your operations, try to lower the fixed costs, either by saving electricity, recycling stationery, keeping a minimum inventory, among other things that can help you reduce your expenses.

c) If the place where it is located is large, you can look for a smaller and more economical one. If it is your property, you can sublet a portion of it and get a fixed income that will help you cope with some expenses.

d) Conduct a survey with customers regarding the services they provide or products they currently sell and on which other services or products they would like to find in their business. This can be an indicator of some niche market that you are not attending and can help you change your turn or venture into the diversification of products or services that may be more profitable soon.

e) Develop a budget of at least the next six months. Be realistic, include your income and monthly fixed expenses. Determine how long you can survive and look for some options to increase your income or lower your costs.

f) Offer promotions and discounts. Remember that the important thing is the flow of money, so although the profits are less than usual, at least the product will sell in a shorter time and you can make the cycle of buying and selling faster, which ultimately will bring a benefit to your company.

g) Treat your customers with respect, if they are regular call them by name or surname, give them a preferential treatment and ask to be recommended. Remember that the recommendations always work more than any other advertising medium and does not cost.

h) Seek advice on administrative, fiscal and financial matters, accountant's associations, chambers of commerce, public and private universities, provide low-cost talks, consultancies and workshops and sometimes as part of their social service to Community.

The important thing is not to abandon your goals. Discuss the options you have, raise the strategies you can follow to cope with the situation you are in and make the necessary decisions. The main thing is to be proactive, that is to act and not to drift, remember the popular wisdom that "shrimp that falls asleep...."

Ethics in Marketing

Marketing is the realization of business activities that direct the flow of goods and services from the producer to the consumer, including the process of planning and execution of conception, pricing, promotion and distribution of ideas, goods, and services to create exchanges that meet the objectives of individuals and organizations.

Marketing ethics includes the principles and standards that guide the behavior of individuals and groups to make marketing decisions. The marketing strategy should consider stakeholders, such as managers, employees, customers, industrial associations, government regulators, business partners, and special groups, all of which contribute to the accepted standards and the expectations of society.

The most basic of these standards have been codified as laws and regulations to encourage companies to adapt to society's expectations about business behavior. The standards of conduct that determine ethics in these activities require that organizations and individuals accept responsibility for their actions and comply with established value systems. However, undue practices that cause or induce error when deciding to buy a product or service are still being carried out and are detrimental to the consumer, such as:

Improper practices in general

Lying about the capabilities of the company, manipulation or misuse of data or information, exploitation of children or vulnerable groups, invasion of privacy,

Anti-competitive activities
a.   Product issues

Misrepresentation of information about products or services, do not disclose product defects, misleading warranties, and do not disclose important product information.

b.   Price-fixing issues

Price deception, price settlement among competitors, fraudulent reimbursement policies, reduce package contents without diminishing their size, abusive behavior.

c.   Distribution issues

Opportunistic behavior among the members of the supply chain, agreements of exclusive distribution, binding contracts, retaining product availability, retaining product or promotional support.

d.   Promotion issues

Advertising of hook articles, false or misleading advertising, false or misleading selling techniques, bribery of vendors or agents of purchases, entertainment, and delivery of gifts, lying.

It is important that to maintain and increase your clientele do not incur any of the above practices, remember that the prestige of the company can be one of the competitive advantages that distinguish it to achieve the fidelity of its customers and the recommendation of the same.

The 5 's, quality method applied to companies and guide to personal development.

This method is called 5 ' s because it is formed by 5 Japanese words with the initial letter S, being the following. Seiri, Seiton, Seiso, Seiketsu and Shitsuke. In companies it is the beginning to have a healthy and comfortable productivity every day of work and fundamental to have a higher productivity. Managing the 5 S program begins with the people, it is important the training for the staff follow good habits of doing things right.

SEIRI.- It is to classify the necessary things from the unnecessary ones in the work area.

SEITON.-It is to fix, order to allow us to easily take things for use.

SEISO.- Itis to clean your workplace completely so that there is no dust on the floor, machines and equipment.

SEIKETSU.- Consists of repeating continuously

Seiri-Seiton-seiso to keep the work area comfortable and productive.

SHITSUKE.- It consists in the training of the personnel since the people must acquire the good work habits and follow the rules in strict form.

In the business and personal area, you can apply the 5 ' S + 1 that believes that all actions are developed as a normal activity, is not a special or additional activity to realize and apply this methodology in our way of life, is simply do what is needing to do, in the place where you live or work. So, the plus 1 in this case would be constant.

Therefore:

1) In relation to things:

  a) Seiri means classification and its purpose is to keep only what is necessary.
  b) Seiton is organization and is concerned with keeping everything in order.
  c) Six is cleanliness and its purpose is to keep everything clean.

2) In relation to yourself:

a) Seiketsu (personal well-being) refers to taking care of your physical and mental health
b) Shitsuke is discipline, maintain reliable behavior.
c) Shikari is constancy, persevering in good habits.
d) Shitsokoku is commitment, go to the end of the tasks.

3) In relation to the company:

a) Seishoo is coordination and refers to acting as a team with peers.
b) Seido is standardization and its purpose is to unify work through standards.

It is important to analyze these principles that seem very simple but can make a big difference, by keeping our house, workplace and ourselves clean, eliminating what is not used either by giving away, selling or disposing of items, repairing what is useful but is broken down or damaged, ordering things that will allow more space and easy to clean, finish the activities that are started, promoting the discipline and creating with this process a better working environment and at home.

Strategic human Resources planning

Strategic planning is aimed at achieving institutional objectives; It is also considered the process of deciding on an organization, its resources and the policies that will guide the achievement of its objectives. About human resources, it is the process of anticipating and preventing the movement of people inward, within and outside the organization.

Benefits:

a) Allows people to be placed in the quantity, quality, and opportunity that the company needs.

b) Allows you to detect opportunities.

c) Reduces consequences of changes and adverse conditions.

d) allows you to allocate resources and make timely decisions.

e) Constitutes a communication framework between the staff.

f) Incorporates individual behavior into group effort.

g) Promotes positive attitude towards change.

h) Provides discipline and formality to business administration.

Importance:

a) Individual. It helps people in the use of their potential.

b) Organizational. Ensures staff disposition in quantity, quality, and opportunity.

c) Environmental.   Improves the environment by providing opportunities for the company and its employees

Objectives:

To optimize the human factor of the company, to ensure in time the necessary template qualitatively and quantitatively; Develop, train, and promote current staff in relation to the future needs of the company; Motivate the human factor of the company, improve the organizational climate, and contribute to maximize the profit of the company

Elements of the strategic plan:

At this point the following elements are considered: identification of key areas of human resources, establishing the human resources mission, conducting a diagnostic analysis of the strengths and weaknesses of the personnel with which it is counted, identifying gaps and Critical areas, determine the target of RR. HH., choice of strategy, establishment of RR. HH policies., formulate action plans and budgeting of human resources, that is to say the amounts that will be required in the future for the payment of salaries, salaries and social benefits.

Process of continuous improvement in the companies, a strategy to improve the quality and efficiency.

Continuous improvement rather than a focus or concept is a strategy and constitutes a series of general action and resource programs to achieve complete objectives, which aims to improve products, services, and processes.

At present the business system is in a process of improvement That itself constitutes an improvement programmed, but to the extent that it is supported by approaches used in world practice, better results will be obtained. An improvement plan requires that the company develop a system that allows:

- Have trained employees to do the job well, control defects, errors and perform different tasks or operations.
- Have motivated employees who work hard and seek to perform the operations in an optimal manner and suggest improvements.
- To have employees with willingness to change, capable and willing to adapt to new situations in the organization.

The application of the improvement methodology requires certain investments. It is possible and desirable to justify such investments in economic terms through the savings and Productivity increases. Some of the tools used include corrective, preventive actions, and the analysis of satisfaction in the members or clients. This is the most effective way to improve quality and efficiency in organizations. In the case of companies, quality management systems, ISO standards and environmental assessment systems are used to achieve the objective of quality. Continuous improvement requires:

- Management support, including: logical organization of the work, identification of the problem and planning, observations and analysis, establishment of objectives to achieve, setting of control indicators..
- Feedback and review of steps in each process. It includes the exhaustive and systematic preparation of the plan, Controlled application of the plan, verification of the application.
- Clarity in the responsibility of each act performed. Verification of the results of the actions carried out and comparison with the objectives.
- To adjust: To analyze the obtained data., to propose alternative of improvement, standardization and consolidation, preparation of the next stage of the plan.

Therefore, the continuous improvement means to improve the standards, establishing at the same time, higher standards, so that once this concept has been established, the maintenance work by the administration or the person responsible for the process, is to ensure that Observe the new standards. When process improvements are made, these will eventually lead to improved quality and productivity, thus avoiding the concern For the results. Whenever a new standard for innovation is implemented, it must be followed by a series of efforts by the process manager and his staff, to maintain and improve it, as a strategic basis for the development of each of the processes that Set up the company.

Companies cannot continue without fully utilizing the intellectual, creative and experience capabilities of all their people. In the same way as a product of social and cultural changes, in companies all have the duty to put the best of themselves for the success of the organization. Their jobs, future and growth possibilities for personal and labor development depend fully on it.

Planning process strategy for micro and small businesses.

The strategic planning process includes the development or revision of the mission and vision of the company, it is important to establish that no matter how small your business is, it must have a purpose and goals, for example: A taco shop can be intended to sell tacos well elaborated, with hygiene, excellent taste and at an affordable price and have as goals to increase their clientele, sell a greater amount of tacos, work double shift, among others.

But how to achieve these goals, a very useful and easy to use tool is the strategic planning methodology. Here are some tips that can help you apply this strategy:

Strategic planning Steps:

a) begins with the definition of its mission (for which it serves its company, which it does), and the vision (where it wants to reach, its goals);

b) In the second term it must identify the threats (competition, costs of raw material, among other external aspects that we cannot control) and opportunities, for example: not to pay taxes for one year in case of tax incorporation, a possible contract.

c) Likewise, to determine the weaknesses (few employees, lack of training, very small local, among other aspects that are a problem of internal character and that if we can change), and to detect the strengths of the business, for example: product of quality, flavor distinctive, good service, good location, personal attention.

d. Generate alternative strategies through thinking about what I can do to achieve my goals by considering the threats, weaknesses, strengths, and opportunities that it already detects.

e. Development of the strategic plan, refers to making decisions about what is going to be done, considering the deadlines, material resources that will be required and who is going to carry it out, for example: you want to expand the business schedule, then extra staff is required to cover the schedule, you know the product or service, it is needed in addition to an updated inventory to cover the possible demand and to make the new timetable known to customers.

F. Development of the tactical plan, refers to how to carry out each activity in detail, i.e. costs, specific time and measures to take, following the example above: for extra staff to change schedules to an employee who already has or hire a new one and train (set deadline for hiring, salary, schedule), about inventory (determine date of the inventory, who will carry it out) and request for missing products or fast displacement (establish how much, when and how to pay), and to make known the new timetable (to make flyers, leaflets, loudspeakers, email, between use of other Media; Who will do it, how much time and cost).

Control and evaluation of results, it is very important that the owner or manager check that the planned actions are being carried out, in time and form, to be able to take the measures or actions that are required at the opportune time. The evaluation of results is realized once the plan has already been started, to know if it works and otherwise make the necessary decisions.

h) Once this process is over, it is repeated with other objectives.

Remember that the strategic planning process is continuing, i.e. never ends, because you must constantly be looking for opportunities to improve the activities and processes that are done in a business and through the application of this administrative tool you can help to consolidate your business and the most important grow on a fixed course, i.e. with a clear goal and with the elements it requires to achieve it.

Cash budget, an indispensable tool to determine the liquidity of a company.

The way a company assigns its resources is a decisive element in evaluating the overall performance of the enterprise. By allocating resources, administrators consider their operations, opportunities, and Impact on the property of the owner or partners, if any. Any major resource allocation decision implies a calculation of how much this decision is worth, regardless of the magnitude of the enterprise.

A project must generate future economic benefits that justify investment; It is also of paramount importance to determine where you will get the money needed to do it, whether for the acquisition of a transport equipment, machinery, land, building, raw material or any other asset that is required.

On the other hand, it is important to know how to deal with the amortization of credit, so that calculations and financial projections must be made. A very simple and used way of knowing the liquidity of the company is making a cash budget, through the method of inputs and outputs.

To prepare it, it is necessary to know all the budgeted cash entries during the period in which the credit will be paid. It is done monthly and includes expected sales in cash, collection to customers, interest receivable and some other possible income to obtain. Total income is subtracted from the total expected expenses in the month, including payment to suppliers, salaries, taxes payable, among other fixed and extraordinary expenses to be made, of course must include the proportional payment of the acquired credit.

Once the subtraction of lower income is made, you get the difference that can be a surplus or a cash shortage. This result will serve to make decisions when determining whether the company will be able to deal with its debts with probable income expected in the same period.

It is appropriate that if the investment is decided to be assessed the actual data and be confronted against the budget, to make the corresponding financial and administrative decisions to correct the results and avoid a catastrophe Not being able to cope with the commitments acquired.

System for the evaluation of the performance in the small business

The evaluation is a practice that has been carried out for a long time, since it is an instinct of the human being to make judgments in any circumstance. Evaluation at work is a formal process to qualify job performance, identifying those who deserve increases or promotions and Detects those who require training (Stoner, 1996:412); So, if there are no well-defined parameters and a structure to carry out this evaluation, erroneous judgments can be made arbitrarily and unjustly.

Modern organizations require that in the workplace results will be obtained to help them achieve success, performance evaluation is a useful tool to measure the overall performance of the worker during the development of his functions in A certain time. It is also a source of information that can provide data to determine the salaries, additional benefits that are given to employees and training that is required. In general, wage-setting is determined by job supply and demand, but it is important to be constantly evaluating employee performance to identify those elements that give their effort and dedication in the work.

In small businesses this issue is not considered important, and by the level of income and organizational structure do not have the capacity to establish a human resources department being these functions performed by the owner, manager or accountant of the company, most of the time without the knowledge necessary to carry them out in an efficient way. Thus, the evaluation is done on a discretionary basis and the results are not always made known to the workers, causing conflicts as generally the staff considers that their work is not suitably rewarded. The employee sees in the amount of the fee a measure of the value of their work, sometimes causing staff with experience and capacity to leave the company by not receiving the benefits expected for their work performance. About training, it is usually considered as an expense and not as an investment, the programs sometimes do not coincide with the needs of the employees and therefore do not improve the performance once they have been carried out.

Thus, it is considered important that the evaluation be carried out in small companies in a simple way and without requiring a lot of time in its elaboration and application. The following is a system that uses parameters for measurement to prevent the evaluation to be very subjective, as usually happens in most small businesses.

The stages of the performance evaluation system can be:

Recognition of employees 'activities, is the objective and practical recognition of what the worker should do in his/her job, is a simple job description that integrates the tasks that are carried out to reach the goals and objectives of the Organization. To integrate a task description, the following data are required: Name of the job, location (area and department), supervisor or immediate head, objective of the post and main activities of the post.

Design of the cedula, the criteria for carrying out the performance evaluation card must correspond to the nature of the tasks that are performed in the company, the parameters to be used, can be among others:

- Training needs can be detected with quality parameters in the Work, knowledge of the job, use of materials and safety at work.

- Salary increases, and prizes are determined with the parameters of quality in the work, speed, knowledge of the job initiative and teamwork.

- Promotion can be established based on quality, job knowledge, initiative, discipline, teamwork, and interpersonal relationships.

It is important to establish points to evaluate each parameter, and here is an example of the Cedula that includes some of the above-mentioned aspects:

General Information:

Employee Name: Work area: Job Title: Monthly Salary: Date:

Punctuality and attendance:

Do you meet the established schedule and your attendance every month?

Accumulates from one to two faults and/or three delays per month

Accumulates up to two delays per month 6 gets to have a delay per month 8 never misses or arrives late without justification 10

Quality at work:

Do you perform accurately, reliably and presentation of the tasks entrusted to you?
His work contains a high error rate 4 requires constant supervision because he makes mistakes 6 usually performs good jobs 8 His works are excellent he makes no mistakes 10

Speed at work

Do you run the jobs that are entrusted to you promptly?
It is slow in delivering jobs 4 regularly delivery on time 6 always delivery in time 8 delivery the work in advance 10

Discipline

Do you abide by the provisions of the superiors for the proper functioning of your work area?
If you can evade instructions 4 manifests disagreement but follow indications 6 sometimes object to instructions 8 Always subject to the instructions received 10

Initiative

Do you show willingness to work on your own, even if your boss isn't here?
No, requires constant invitations to work 4 if, only sometimes needs recommendations 6 Yes, it is never necessary to remind him of his work 8 if, in addition it proposes improvements in the work 10

Interpersonal relationships

Do you show openness to interpersonal relationships? with their peers and superiors?
Rejects the deal with his mates 4 relationships are acceptable 6 it is usually friendly with heads and companions 8 keeps excellent deal with all 10

Use of materials and equipment
Do you properly use the equipment, materials and resources assigned to perform your tasks?
Unreasonably spends material and equipment 4 occasionally shows faults in the care of the material and equipment 6 strives to retain material and equipment 8 strives to care for materials 10

    Total points:
    Comments:
    Strong areas:
    Weak areas:
    Name and signature of supervisor signature of employee

Application of the identification card.
The assessment should be fair and qualify according to the result you get during your worker's
performance, each question must have several responses options through a point scale that represents the level of productivity. Once the points are marked, it is necessary to add them to obtain the level of productivity of the worker. Some policies of the implementing procedure are, for example: Evaluating twice a year, new-income staff the first time at six months, prior to evaluation, obtaining the information necessary to evaluate each parameter; In case of having the two outstanding evaluations, a promotion or prize can be originated, on the contrary if deficiencies are found, it can be considered the programming of necessary training courses.
Feedback with collaborators. It is intended to talk with employees about their results through an interview that must be private and individually.

The importance of feedback is that a clear idea should be given to the appraised about their performance, observing their strengths and weaknesses, to match them with the expected performance patterns. Some employees may not realize that they are not reaching the expectations or think that everything is acceptable because no one has ever discussed the problem with them (Maddux, 1991:51).

Establishment of commitments. They must be mutually agreed in order not to exercise authority and to generate greater responsibility in the employee. It is advisable to write down the Commitments and the date of compliance, to keep track of it.

Presentation of results. It is carried out by means of the emptying of the data obtained in the evaluation by areas, to know in which, they require greater support, by means of the sum of the results obtained by each parameter.

Finally, the importance of evaluating performance in a company is that based on the results obtained it is possible to diagnose training needs and to serve as a basis for rewarding employees with higher scores through salary increases, promotions, protection programs, business cards, opportunities for personal growth; Among other aspects, that will motivate the staff through a process that will determine benefits for the evaluated and It will result in the productivity of the company by having motivated workers and with the desire to achieve the objectives that the company establishes. Otherwise, there is a risk that employees who meet the proposed standards will leave the company causing expenses related to the search, selection, induction, and training of new employees, among others.

Suggestions for motivating staff in the company

Motivation is an impulse that allows us to maintain a certain continuity in the action that brings us closer to the attainment of a goal and that once achieved, will satisfy a need, also it is considered that it is the combination between the desires and energies of the person to reach a goal. This behavior requires several elements:

- Effort – refers to the magnitude or intensity of the behavior that is exhibited to reach a goal either personal or work.

- Persistence – refers to sustained effort to achieve a goal.

- Direction—refers to whether the effort and persistence go in the right way

Work Motivation Techniques:

- Promotion at work. As a reward for achieving proposed goals.

- Wage policy. Include concepts of bonuses, achievement of goals, among others.

- Working environment. Refers to the physical environment (tools and equipment in good condition, safety, ventilation, lighting, etc.) and medium Social (fellowship, work teams, communication, among others).

- Valuation Man-job position. To consider the personal skills and their performance in relation to the responsibility and complexity of the tasks according to the position.

Means to evaluate the motivation in the company:

The observation and appraisal of workers 'attitudes, questionnaires or lists of questions, interviews, surveys, analysis of working conditions.

Suggestions to encourage job motivation:

- Involve staff in decision-making according to their ability.

- Keep staff informed of the tasks to be performed and their rewards.

- To maintain an "open door" policy and to see equity in reward allocation.

- Develop a care attitude by setting goals so that they are achievable.

- Listen and know the employees to know their expectations and aspects that motivate them

- Invite them to give suggestions and offer constructive criticism.

- Recognize good performance and manage positive motivation.

- Describe to others what is expected of them

- Maintain high standards of execution

Remember that to motivate others we must start with ourselves, consider that the best way to keep employee motivation is to understand what motivates them and to recognize that keeping others motivated is a process, not a task.

Competitive advantage in human resources through strategic planning.

The goal of strategic planning is to have a client-focused organization, the market and the competition, sustaining a competitive advantage that generates value.

For this, it is necessary to develop a tactical planning that is the basis for strategic decision making, and consider the nature and direction of the business, the principles under which it is intended to operate and the direction in which it should be advanced.

On the other hand, strategic planning is based on intuition and data analysis, here is clearly defined what you want, how and when it will be done and who will be the manager, includes goals with a time horizon of 1 to 3 years and envisages action plans, budgets, and programs.

Regarding the strategic planning of human Resources, the following aspects should be considered:

A. Long-term performance aspiration

B. Sharing the beliefs of ¨ things we will do/we won't do"
C. Capabilities that distinguish us and differentiate us

It is necessary to consider absenteeism, which is the duration of lost working time when the employee does not show up for work. Represents a cost to the company in the percentage of workforce availability.

Rotation of personnel, which is the result of the outputs and inputs of others to replace them. They obey: renunciations, layoffs, promotions,

Transfers, every movement causes the company to spend in the areas of recruitment, selection, training and disconnection.

The elements of the human resources strategic plan should be: Identification of key areas of human resources, determining the mission of human resources, analysis of strengths, opportunities, weaknesses, and threats (SWOT), identification of gaps and areas Criticism, determination of objective of the area, choice of strategy, establishment of policies, formulation of action plans, budgeting of human resources to be required according to the plans of the company in the future.

For its part, the advantages of establishing the strategic plan in this area, among others, are:

1) Individual appearance. It helps people in the use of their potential.
2) Organizational aspect. Ensures staff disposition in quantity, quality, and opportunity.
3) Environmental aspect. It improves the environment providing opportunities for the company and its employees, optimizes the human factor of the company, ensures in time the necessary template qualitatively and quantitatively, contributes to develop, form, and promote the current staff, in relation to the future needs of the company, it manages to motivate the human factor of the company and to improve the climate Organization, maximizes the profit of the company.

Bibliography

Chiavenato, I (2007). Human Resources Administration, 8th. Ed. Mexico: McGraw-Hill.

Chiavenato, I (2009) Organizational behavior, 2 °. Ed. Mexico: McGraw-Hill.

Dessler, G. (2009) Human Resources Administration, 11th. Ed., Mexico: Pearson

INEGI, (2009) Micro, Small, medium and large companies, stratification of the establishments, economic censuses, Mexico.

Kotler, P., Keller, K. (2009), marketing Director, 12th. E. Mexico: Pearson.

Kotler, P. (2011), Marketing According to Kotler, Mexico: Paidos.

Pedraza, O. (2014),; Business Plan model for Micro and small Business, Mexico: Patria.

Robbins, S., Judge T. (2013). Organizational behavior, 15th. E., Mexico: Pearson.

Valencia, J.R. (2011). Small and Medium Business Administration, Mexico: Cengage Learning

Werther W., D.K. (2013). Human Resources Administration, 7th. Ed., Mexico: McGraw-Hill

Electronic references
www.inmujeres.gob.mx
www.inegi.gob.mx
www.economia.gob.mx
www.sectur.gob.mx

www.ingramcontent.com/pod-product-compliance
Lightning Source LLC
Chambersburg PA
CBHW072047230526
45468CB00019B/682